THE STANDARD EDITION
OF THE COMPLETE PSYCHOLOGICAL WORKS OF

ROEE ROSEN

Translated from the German under the General Editorship of

JAMES STRACHEY

In Collaboration with

ANNA FREUD

Assisted by

ALIX STRACHEY and ALAN TYSON

Editorial Assistant: ANGELA RICHARDS

VOLUME I

(1886–1889)

Psycho-Jew

The Complete Unpublished Novel
with an Introduction Concerning Former Super-Villains
and the Menstruation of Jewish Men

by

JOANNA FÜHRER-HASFARI

LONDON

THE HOGARTH PRESS

AND THE INSTITUTE OF PSYCHO-ANALYSIS

THE STANDARD EDITION
OF THE COMPLETE PSYCHOLOGICAL WORKS OF

ROEE ROSEN

Translated from the German under the General Editorship of

JAMES STRACHEY

In Collaboration with

ANNA FREUD

Assisted by

ALIX STRACHEY and ALAN TYSON

VOLUME II

(1893–1895)

Preverbal Reflections

LONDON
THE HOGARTH PRESS
AND THE INSTITUTE OF PSYCHO-ANALYSIS

THE STANDARD EDITION
OF THE COMPLETE PSYCHOLOGICAL WORKS OF

ROEE ROSEN

Translated from the German under the General Editorship of

JAMES STRACHEY

In Collaboration with

ANNA FREUD

Assisted by

ALIX STRACHEY and ALAN TYSON

VOLUME III

(1893–1899)

How to Become Several Women

LONDON

THE HOGARTH PRESS

AND THE INSTITUTE OF PSYCHO-ANALYSIS

THE STANDARD EDITION
OF THE COMPLETE PSYCHOLOGICAL WORKS OF

ROEE ROSEN

Translated from the German under the General Editorship of

JAMES STRACHEY

In Collaboration with

ANNA FREUD

Assisted by

ALIX STRACHEY and ALAN TYSON

VOLUME IV

(1900)

Planning the Past

With an Appendix on Palestine

LONDON

THE HOGARTH PRESS

AND THE INSTITUTE OF PSYCHO-ANALYSIS

THE STANDARD EDITION
OF THE COMPLETE PSYCHOLOGICAL WORKS OF

ROEE ROSEN

Translated from the German under the General Editorship of

JAMES STRACHEY

In Collaboration with

ANNA FREUD

Assisted by

ALIX STRACHEY and ALAN TYSON

VOLUME V

(1900–1901)

Health Problems Induced by Autobiographies

LONDON

THE HOGARTH PRESS

AND THE INSTITUTE OF PSYCHO-ANALYSIS

THE STANDARD EDITION
OF THE COMPLETE PSYCHOLOGICAL WORKS OF

ROEE ROSEN

Translated from the German under the General Editorship of

JAMES STRACHEY

In Collaboration with

ANNA FREUD

Assisted by

ALIX STRACHEY and ALAN TYSON

VOLUME VI

(1901)

Longing to Become a Sardine
Longing to Become a Beetle
Gaining the Trust of Insects
and
Other Childhood Designs

LONDON

THE HOGARTH PRESS

AND THE INSTITUTE OF PSYCHO-ANALYSIS

THE STANDARD EDITION
OF THE COMPLETE PSYCHOLOGICAL WORKS OF

ROEE ROSEN

Translated from the German under the General Editorship of

JAMES STRACHEY

In Collaboration with

ANNA FREUD

Assisted by

ALIX STRACHEY and ALAN TYSON

VOLUME VII

(1901–1905)

The Menacing Mattress
Infantile Magic
Nausea Stirred by Beauty
Understanding Money
and
Other Childhood Memoirs

LONDON

THE HOGARTH PRESS

AND THE INSTITUTE OF PSYCHO-ANALYSIS

THE STANDARD EDITION
OF THE COMPLETE PSYCHOLOGICAL WORKS OF

ROEE ROSEN

Translated from the German under the General Editorship of

JAMES STRACHEY

In Collaboration with

ANNA FREUD

Assisted by

ALIX STRACHEY and ALAN TYSON

VOLUME VIII

(1905)

Victimhood Jokes

With an Appendix on Poland

LONDON

THE HOGARTH PRESS

AND THE INSTITUTE OF PSYCHO-ANALYSIS

THE STANDARD EDITION
OF THE COMPLETE PSYCHOLOGICAL WORKS OF

ROEE ROSEN

Translated from the German under the General Editorship of

JAMES STRACHEY

In Collaboration with

ANNA FREUD

Assisted by

ALIX STRACHEY and ALAN TYSON

VOLUME IX

(1906–1908)

My Failure as a Stool

LONDON

THE HOGARTH PRESS

AND THE INSTITUTE OF PSYCHO-ANALYSIS

THE STANDARD EDITION
OF THE COMPLETE PSYCHOLOGICAL WORKS OF

ROEE ROSEN

Translated from the German under the General Editorship of

JAMES STRACHEY

In Collaboration with

ANNA FREUD

Assisted by

ALIX STRACHEY and ALAN TYSON

VOLUME X

(1909)

A Guided Journey
Inside My Grave

LONDON

THE HOGARTH PRESS

AND THE INSTITUTE OF PSYCHO-ANALYSIS

THE STANDARD EDITION
OF THE COMPLETE PSYCHOLOGICAL WORKS OF

ROEE ROSEN

Translated from the German under the General Editorship of

JAMES STRACHEY

In Collaboration with

ANNA FREUD

Assisted by

ALIX STRACHEY and ALAN TYSON

VOLUME XI

(1910)

On Salvaging and Nursing Old and Dying Jokes

and

A Collection of Unfunny Jokes

LONDON

THE HOGARTH PRESS

AND THE INSTITUTE OF PSYCHO-ANALYSIS

THE STANDARD EDITION
OF THE COMPLETE PSYCHOLOGICAL WORKS OF

ROEE ROSEN

Translated from the German under the General Editorship of

JAMES STRACHEY

In Collaboration with

ANNA FREUD

Assisted by

ALIX STRACHEY and ALAN TYSON

VOLUME XII

(1911–1913)

A New Lexicon of Armpits and Genitalia Physiognomy *and* Papers on Technique

LONDON
THE HOGARTH PRESS
AND THE INSTITUTE OF PSYCHO-ANALYSIS

THE STANDARD EDITION
OF THE COMPLETE PSYCHOLOGICAL WORKS OF

ROEE ROSEN

Translated from the German under the General Editorship of

JAMES STRACHEY

In Collaboration with

ANNA FREUD

Assisted by

ALIX STRACHEY and ALAN TYSON

VOLUME XIII

(1913–1914)

Pretending to Be Yourself
Nestling in Waste
Garbage and Waste
Ololon Forgotten
and
Other Current Works

LONDON
THE HOGARTH PRESS
AND THE INSTITUTE OF PSYCHO-ANALYSIS

THE STANDARD EDITION
OF THE COMPLETE PSYCHOLOGICAL WORKS OF

ROEE ROSEN

Translated from the German under the General Editorship of

JAMES STRACHEY

In Collaboration with

ANNA FREUD

Assisted by

ALIX STRACHEY and ALAN TYSON

VOLUME XIV

(1914–1916)

The Eruption of the Great War, Unnoticed

LONDON

THE HOGARTH PRESS

AND THE INSTITUTE OF PSYCHO-ANALYSIS

THE STANDARD EDITION
OF THE COMPLETE PSYCHOLOGICAL WORKS OF

ROEE ROSEN

Translated from the German under the General Editorship of

JAMES STRACHEY

In Collaboration with

ANNA FREUD

Assisted by

ALIX STRACHEY and ALAN TYSON

VOLUME XV

(1915–1916)

Tongues and Armpits: A Psycho-Political History

(PARTS I and II)

LONDON
THE HOGARTH PRESS
AND THE INSTITUTE OF PSYCHO-ANALYSIS

THE STANDARD EDITION
OF THE COMPLETE PSYCHOLOGICAL WORKS OF

ROEE ROSEN

Translated from the German under the General Editorship of

JAMES STRACHEY

In Collaboration with

ANNA FREUD

Assisted by

ALIX STRACHEY and ALAN TYSON

VOLUME XVI

(1916–1917)

The Complete History of Russia in Jokes

The Incomplete Opus by Maxim Komar-Myshkin
An Annotated Revolution Edition

LONDON

THE HOGARTH PRESS

AND THE INSTITUTE OF PSYCHO-ANALYSIS

THE STANDARD EDITION
OF THE COMPLETE PSYCHOLOGICAL WORKS OF

ROEE ROSEN

Translated from the German under the General Editorship of

JAMES STRACHEY

In Collaboration with

ANNA FREUD

Assisted by

ALIX STRACHEY and ALAN TYSON

VOLUME XVII
(1917–1919)

The Geography and Tribes of the Confines of My Room

A Pandemic Quarantine Edition

LONDON
THE HOGARTH PRESS
AND THE INSTITUTE OF PSYCHO-ANALYSIS

THE STANDARD EDITION
OF THE COMPLETE PSYCHOLOGICAL WORKS OF

ROEE ROSEN

Translated from the German under the General Editorship of

JAMES STRACHEY

In Collaboration with

ANNA FREUD

Assisted by

ALIX STRACHEY and ALAN TYSON

VOLUME XVIII

(1920–1922)

How to Hide Your Pains From Yourself

and

Other Works

LONDON
THE HOGARTH PRESS
AND THE INSTITUTE OF PSYCHO-ANALYSIS

THE STANDARD EDITION
OF THE COMPLETE PSYCHOLOGICAL WORKS OF

ROEE ROSEN

Translated from the German under the General Editorship of

JAMES STRACHEY

In Collaboration with

ANNA FREUD

Assisted by

ALIX STRACHEY and ALAN TYSON

VOLUME XIX

(1923–1925)

The Kafka Companion to Wellness

with an Appendix on His Death

LONDON

THE HOGARTH PRESS

AND THE INSTITUTE OF PSYCHO-ANALYSIS

THE STANDARD EDITION
OF THE COMPLETE PSYCHOLOGICAL WORKS OF

ROEE ROSEN

Translated from the German under the General Editorship of

JAMES STRACHEY

In Collaboration with

ANNA FREUD

Assisted by

ALIX STRACHEY and ALAN TYSON

VOLUME XX

(1925–1926)

The Unattainable Ideal of Becoming Ever Smaller

LONDON
THE HOGARTH PRESS
AND THE INSTITUTE OF PSYCHO-ANALYSIS

THE STANDARD EDITION
OF THE COMPLETE PSYCHOLOGICAL WORKS OF

ROEE ROSEN

Translated from the German under the General Editorship of

JAMES STRACHEY

In Collaboration with

ANNA FREUD

Assisted by

ALIX STRACHEY and ALAN TYSON

VOLUME XXI

(1927–1931)

Sewer Mansions of Psycho-Jew

and

Other Unfinished Tales

with

Maps of the Secret Tunnels of the Kunsthistorisches Museum in Vienna, and of the Sewage System of Berlin

LONDON

THE HOGARTH PRESS

AND THE INSTITUTE OF PSYCHO-ANALYSIS

THE STANDARD EDITION
OF THE COMPLETE PSYCHOLOGICAL WORKS OF

ROEE ROSEN

Translated from the German under the General Editorship of

JAMES STRACHEY

In Collaboration with

ANNA FREUD

Assisted by

ALIX STRACHEY and ALAN TYSON

VOLUME XXII

(1932–1936)

How They Took Her from the Playground, Leaving the Children Behind, Unaware

LONDON

THE HOGARTH PRESS

AND THE INSTITUTE OF PSYCHO-ANALYSIS

THE STANDARD EDITION
OF THE COMPLETE PSYCHOLOGICAL WORKS OF

ROEE ROSEN

Translated from the German under the General Editorship of

JAMES STRACHEY

In Collaboration with

ANNA FREUD

Assisted by

ALIX STRACHEY and ALAN TYSON

VOLUME XXIII

(1937–1939)

The Horror of Becoming a Frog Again

and

Other Texts

on Curses and Remissions

LONDON

THE HOGARTH PRESS

AND THE INSTITUTE OF PSYCHO-ANALYSIS

THE STANDARD EDITION
OF THE COMPLETE PSYCHOLOGICAL WORKS OF

ROEE ROSEN

Translated from the German under the General Editorship of

JAMES STRACHEY

In Collaboration with

ANNA FREUD

Assisted by

ALIX STRACHEY and ALAN TYSON

Editorial Assistant: ANGELA RICHARDS

VOLUME XXIV

Confessions on My Confessions

LONDON

THE HOGARTH PRESS

AND THE INSTITUTE OF PSYCHO-ANALYSIS

THE STANDARD EDITION
OF THE COMPLETE PSYCHOLOGICAL WORKS OF

ROEE ROSEN

VOLUME I

(1886–1889)

Psycho-Jew

The Complete Unpublished Novel
with an Introduction Concerning Former Super-Villains
and the Menstruation of Jewish Men

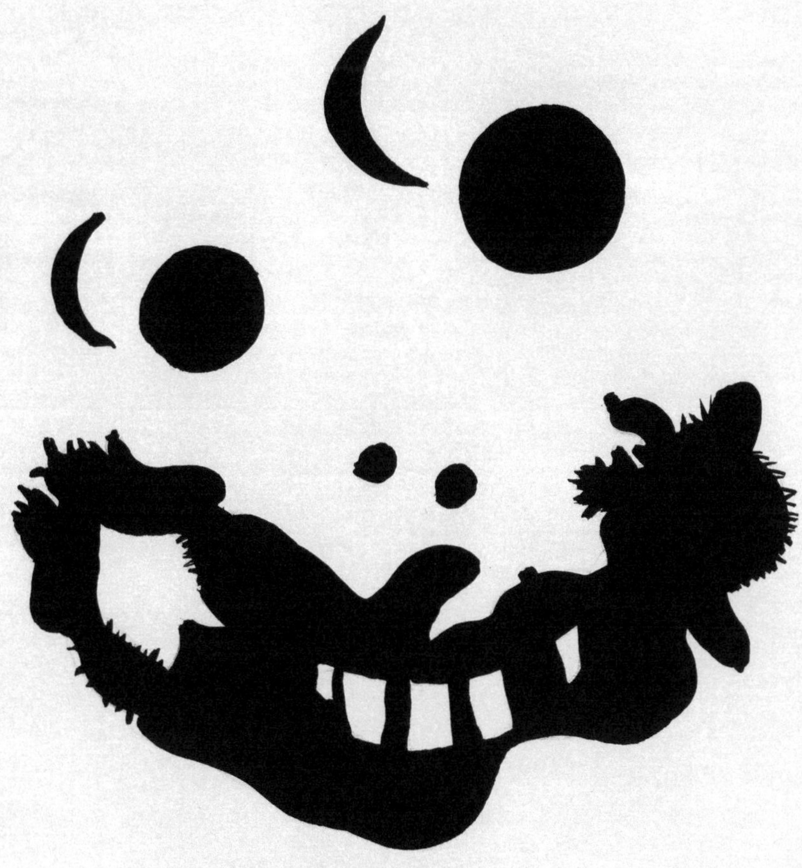

THE HOGARTH PRESS
AND THE INSTITUTE OF PSYCHO-ANALYSIS

THE STANDARD EDITION
OF THE COMPLETE PSYCHOLOGICAL WORKS OF

ROSE ROSEN

VOLUME II
(1893–1895)

Preverbal Reflections

THE HOGARTH PRESS
AND THE INSTITUTE OF PSYCHO-ANALYSIS

THE STANDARD EDITION
OF THE COMPLETE PSYCHOLOGICAL WORKS OF

REESE NOOR

VOLUME III
(1893–1899)

How to Be Several Women

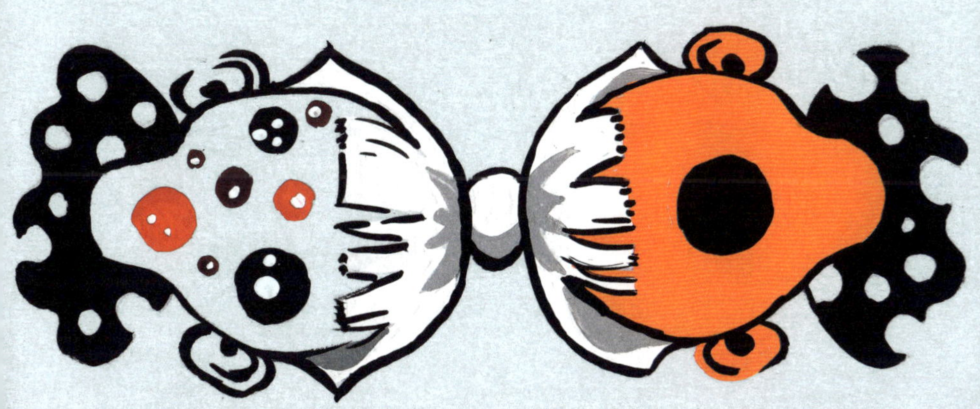

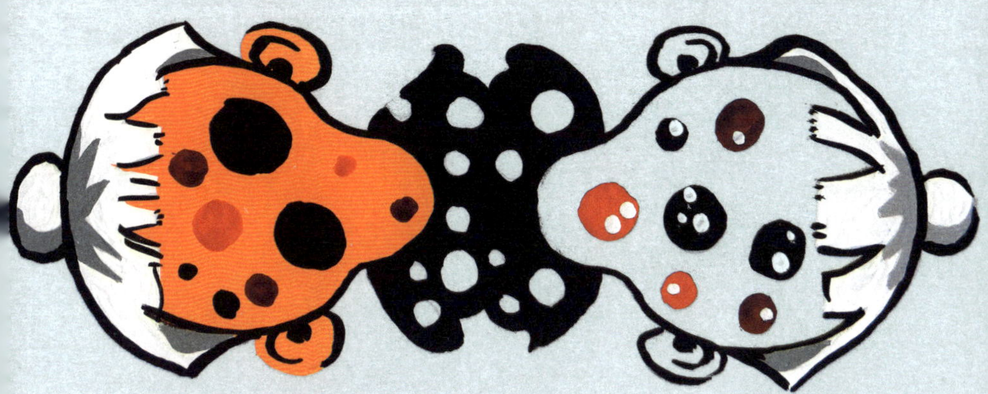

THE HOGARTH PRESS
AND THE INSTITUTE OF PSYCHO-ANALYSIS

THE STANDARD EDITION
OF THE COMPLETE PSYCHOLOGICAL WORKS OF

NOOR REESE

VOLUME IV
(1900)

Planning the Past

With an Appendix on Palestine

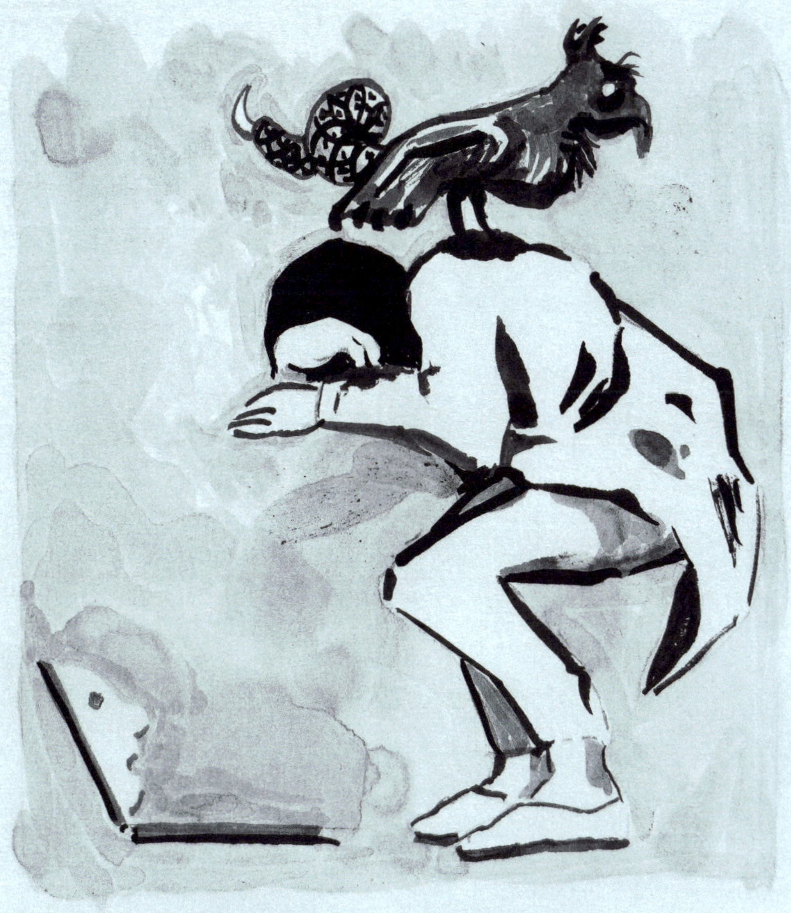

THE HOGARTH PRESS
AND THE INSTITUTE OF PSYCHO-ANALYSIS

THE STANDARD EDITION
OF THE COMPLETE PSYCHOLOGICAL WORKS OF

ENOS SNEER

VOLUME V

(1900–1901)

Memory Problems
Induced by Autobiographies

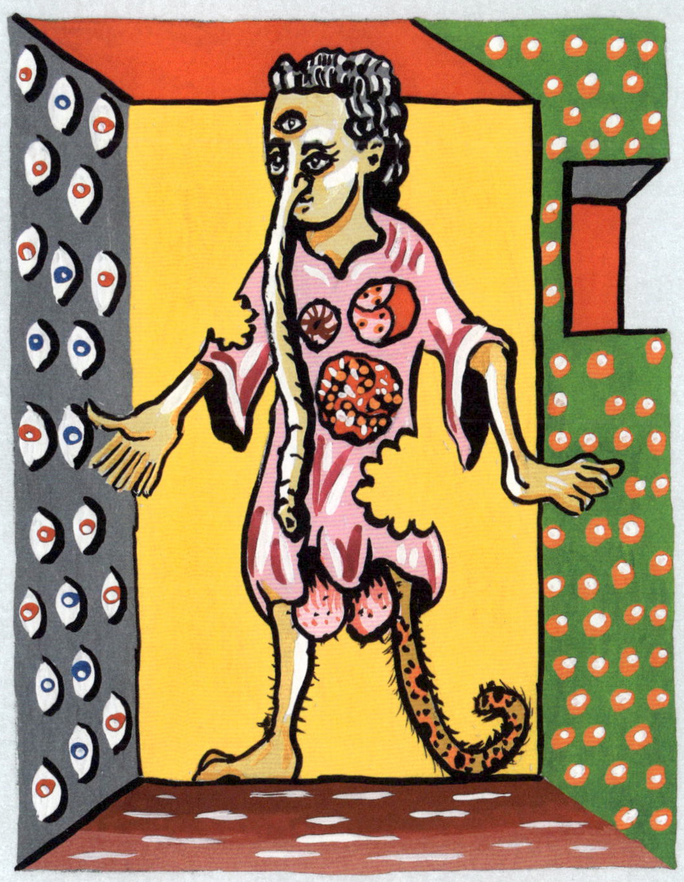

THE HOGARTH PRESS

AND THE INSTITUTE OF PSYCHO-ANALYSIS

THE STANDARD EDITION
OF THE COMPLETE PSYCHOLOGICAL WORKS OF

ROSS ENSOR

VOLUME VI

(1901)

Longing to Become a Sardine
and
Gaining the Trust of Insects

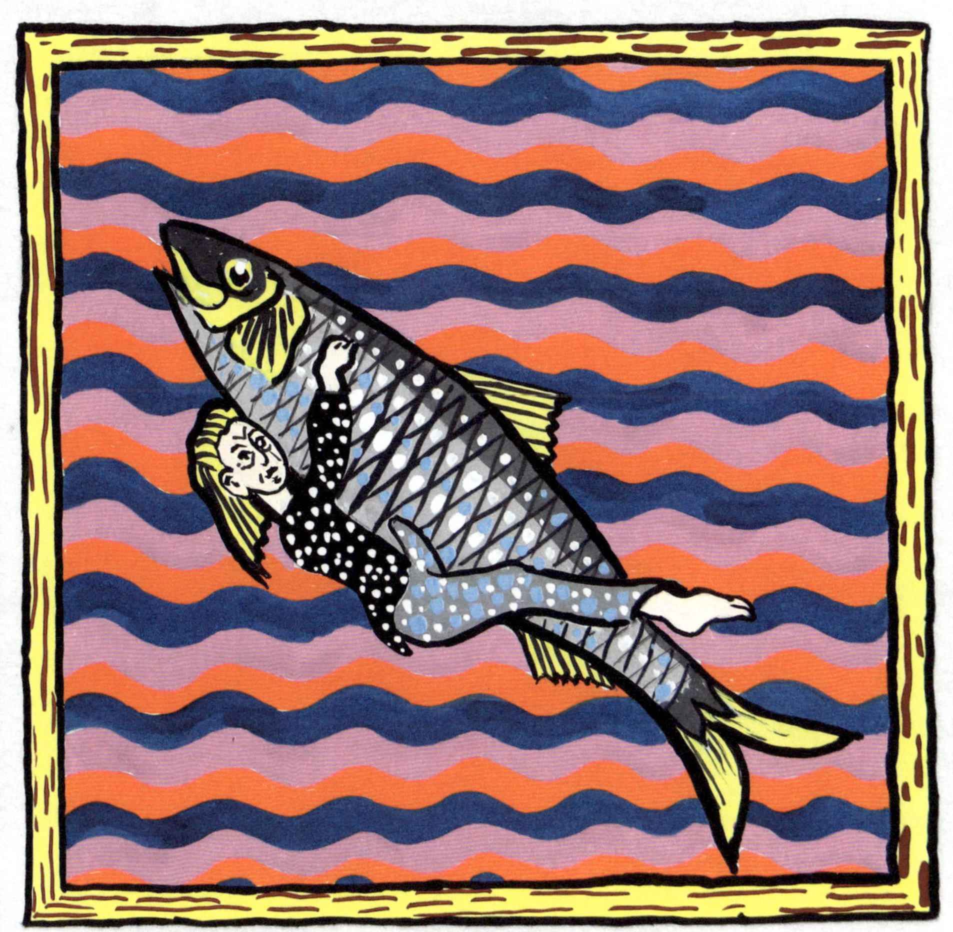

THE HOGARTH PRESS

THE STANDARD EDITION
OF THE COMPLETE PSYCHIC WORKS OF

RORO SEEN

VOLUME VII
(1901–1905)

The Menacing Mattress
Infantile Magic
and
Other Childhood Memoirs

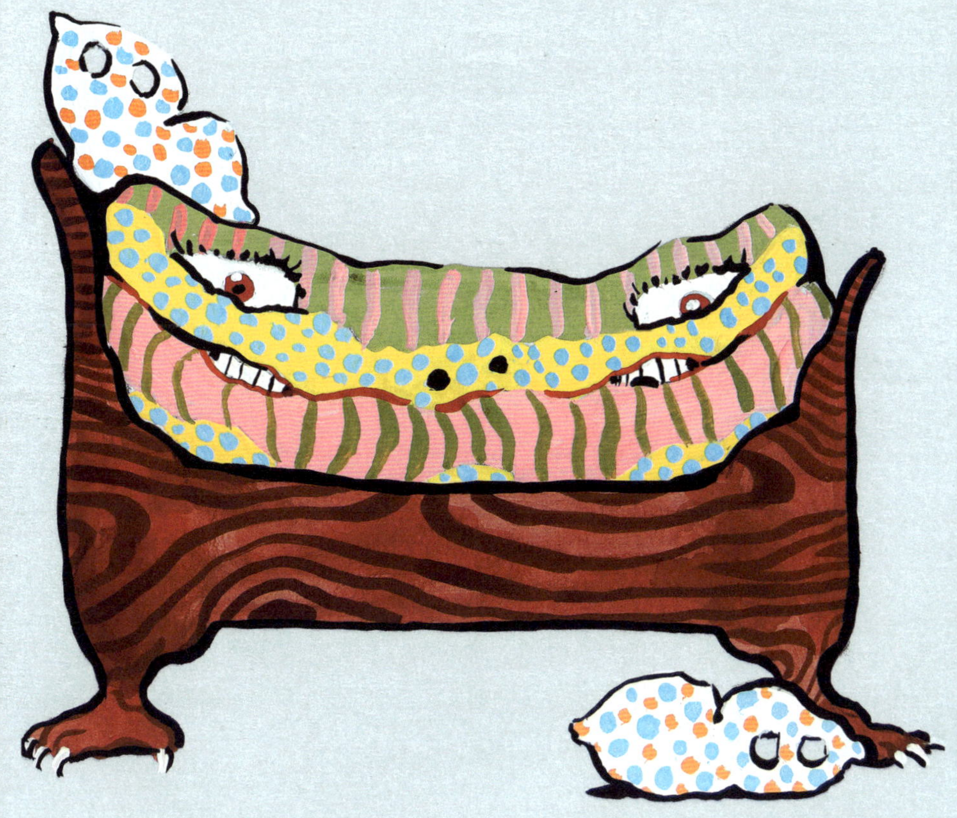

THE HOGARTH PRESS
AND THE INSTITUTE OF PSYCHOS

THE STANDARD EDITION
OF THE COMPLETE PSYCHOLOGICAL WORKS OF

ORSON EERIE

VOLUME VIII

(1905)

Victimhood Jokes

With an Appendix on Poland

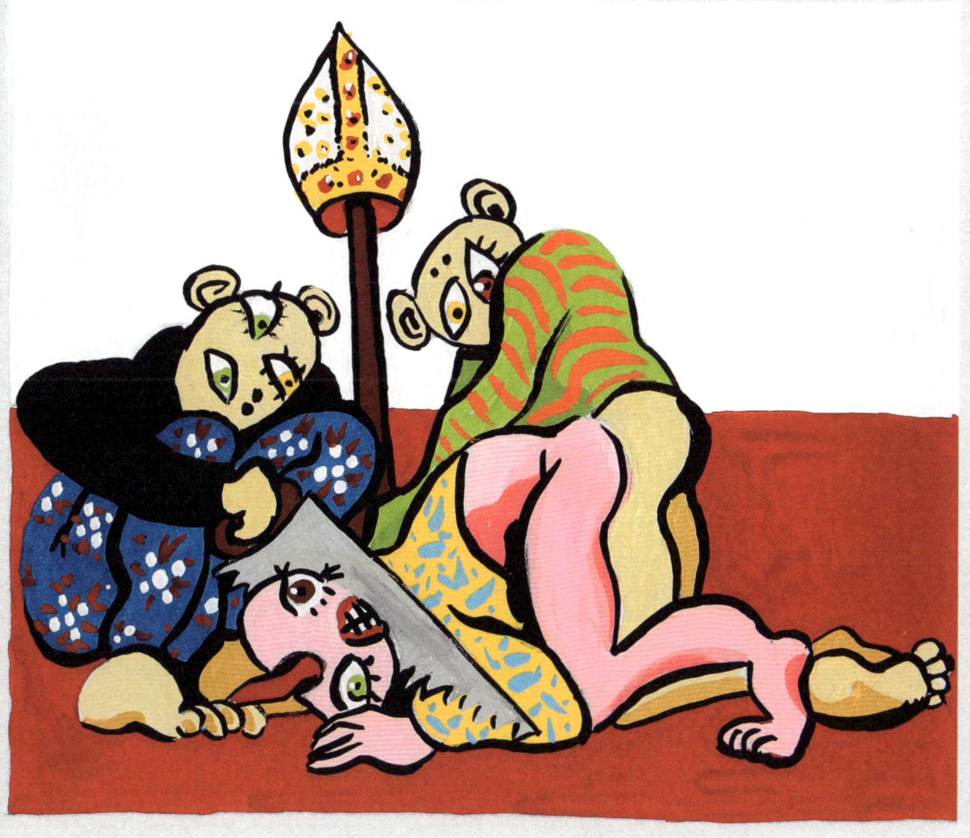

THE HOGARTH PRESS

AND THE INSTITUTE OF PSYCHO-ANALYSIS

THE STANDARD EDITION
OF THE COMPLETE PSYCHOLOGICAL WORKS OF

RROSE SORE

VOLUME IX

(1906–1908)

My Failure as a Stool

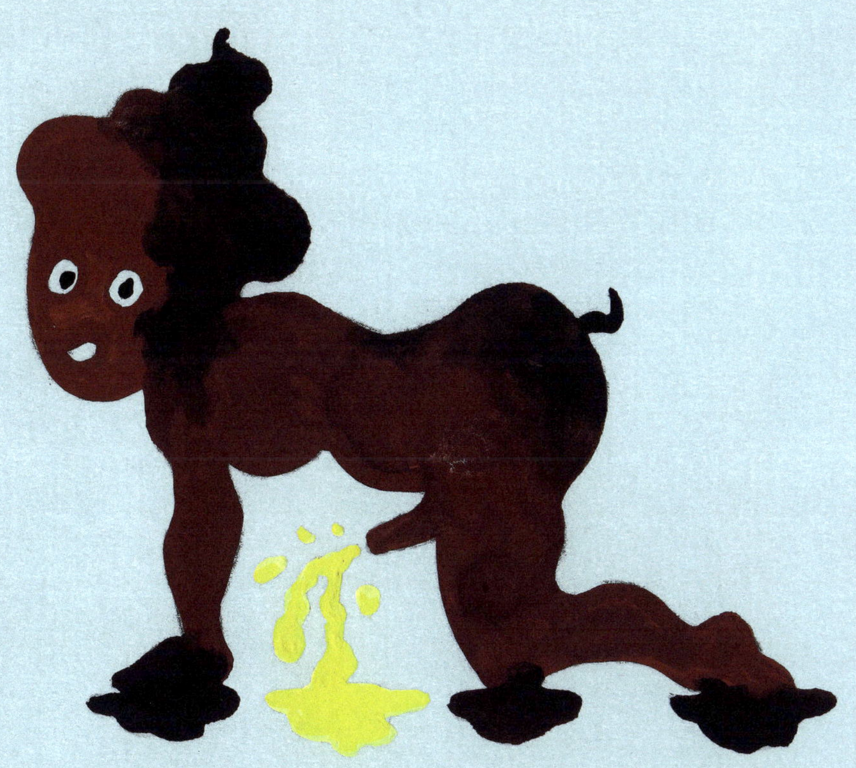

THE HOGARTH PRESS

AND THE INSTITUTE OF PSYCHO-ANALYSIS

THE STANDARD EDITION
OF THE COMPLETE PSYCHOLOGICAL WORKS OF

ROEE ROSEN

VOLUME X

(1909)

A Guided Journey Inside My Grave

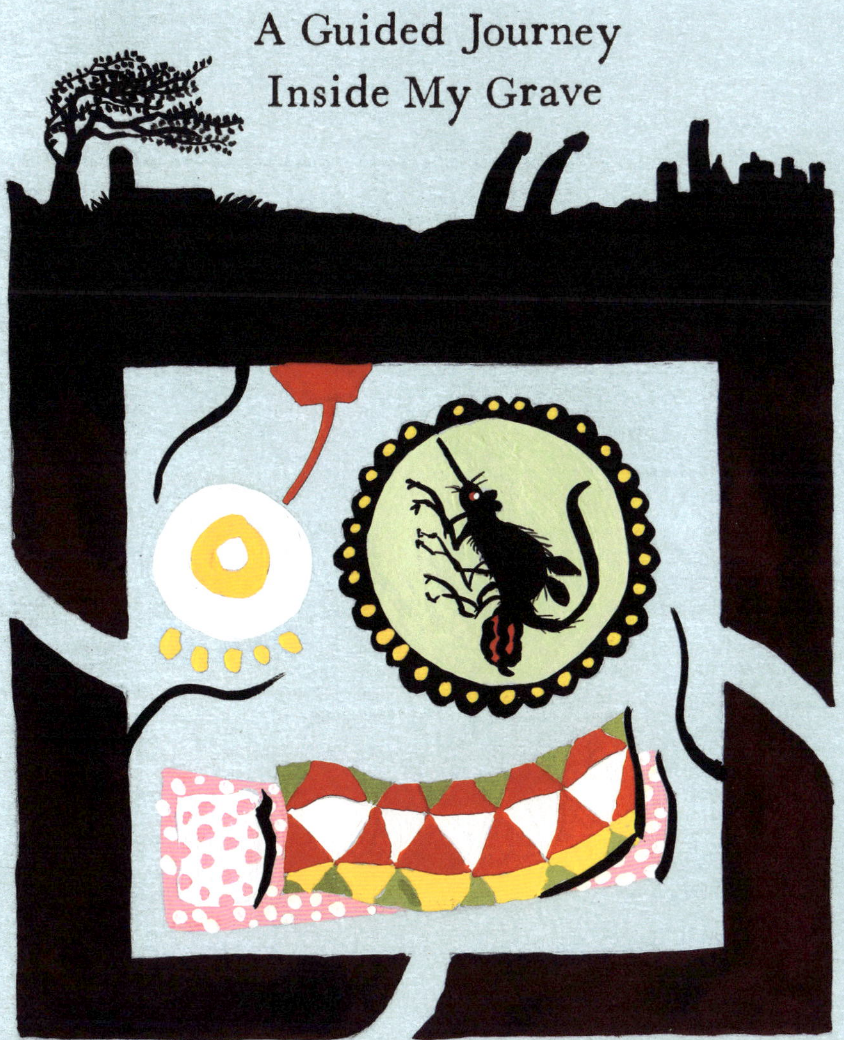

THE EARTH PRESS

THE DARNED EDITION
OF THE COMPLETE PATHOLOGICAL WORKS OF

NURSE ROSIE

VOLUME XI

(1910)

Nursing Dying Jokes

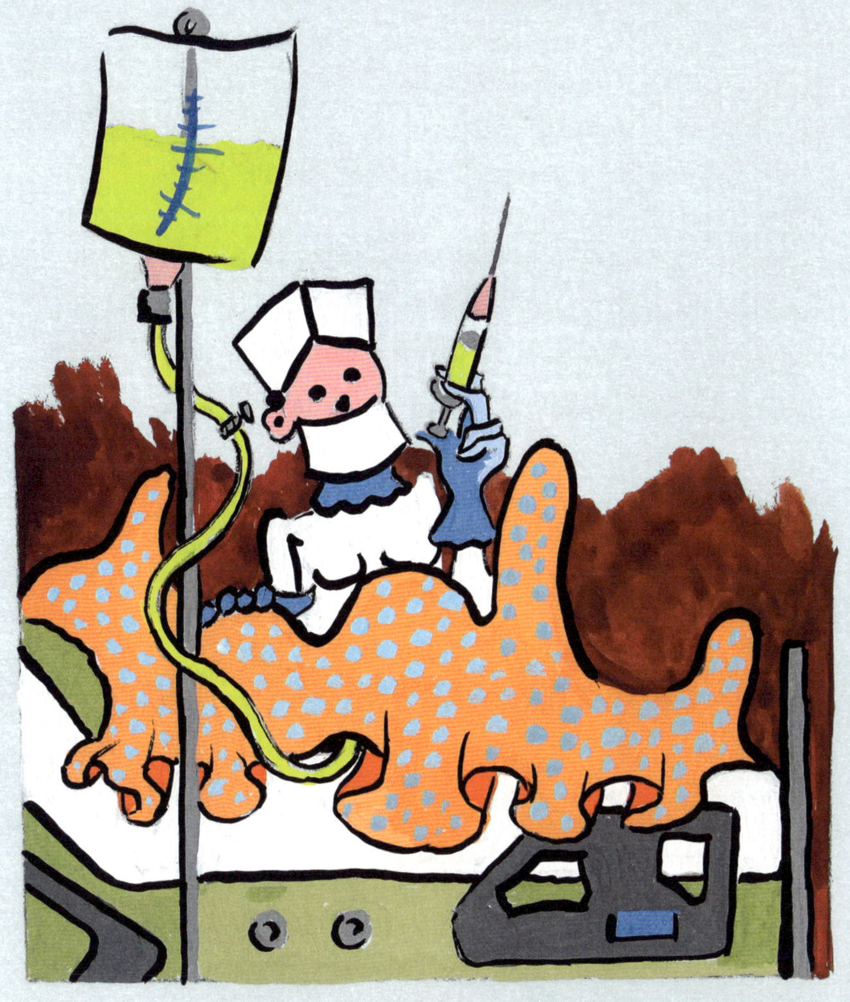

THE HOGARTH PRESS

AND THE INSTITUTE OF PSYCHO-ANALYSIS

THE STANDARD EDITION

O O OO O

EROS RENO

VOLUME XII

(1911–1913)

Armpits and Genitalia Physiognomy

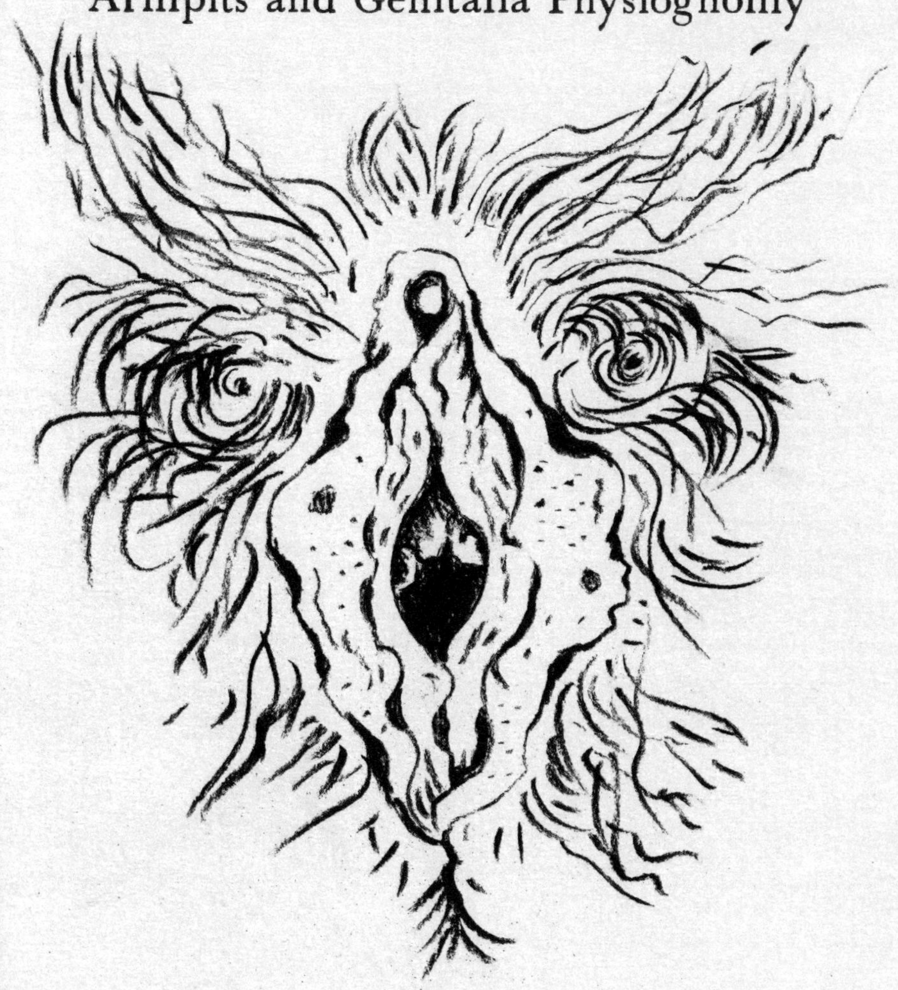

THE HOGARTH PRESS

AND THE INSTITUTE OF PSYCHO-ANALYSIS

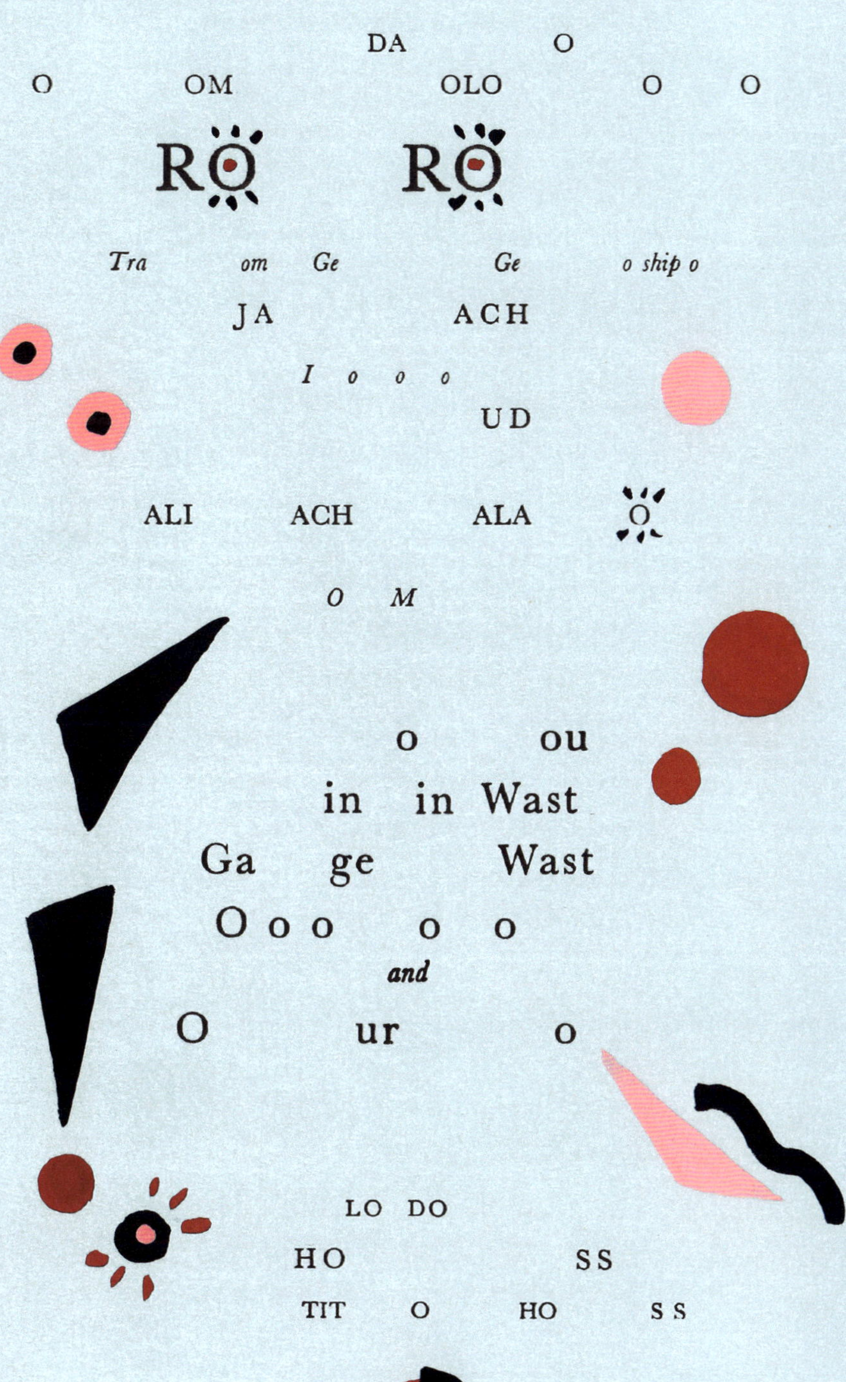
DA O
O OM OLO O O
RO RO
Tra om Ge Ge o ship o
JA ACH
I o o o
UD
ALI ACH ALA O
O M
o ou
in in Wast
Ga ge Wast
O o o o o
and
O ur o
LO DO
HO SS
TIT O HO S S

THE STANDARD EDITION
OF THE COMPLETE PSYCHOLOGICAL WORKS OF

SOREN OREO

VOLUME XIV

(1914–1916)

The Great War, Unnoticed

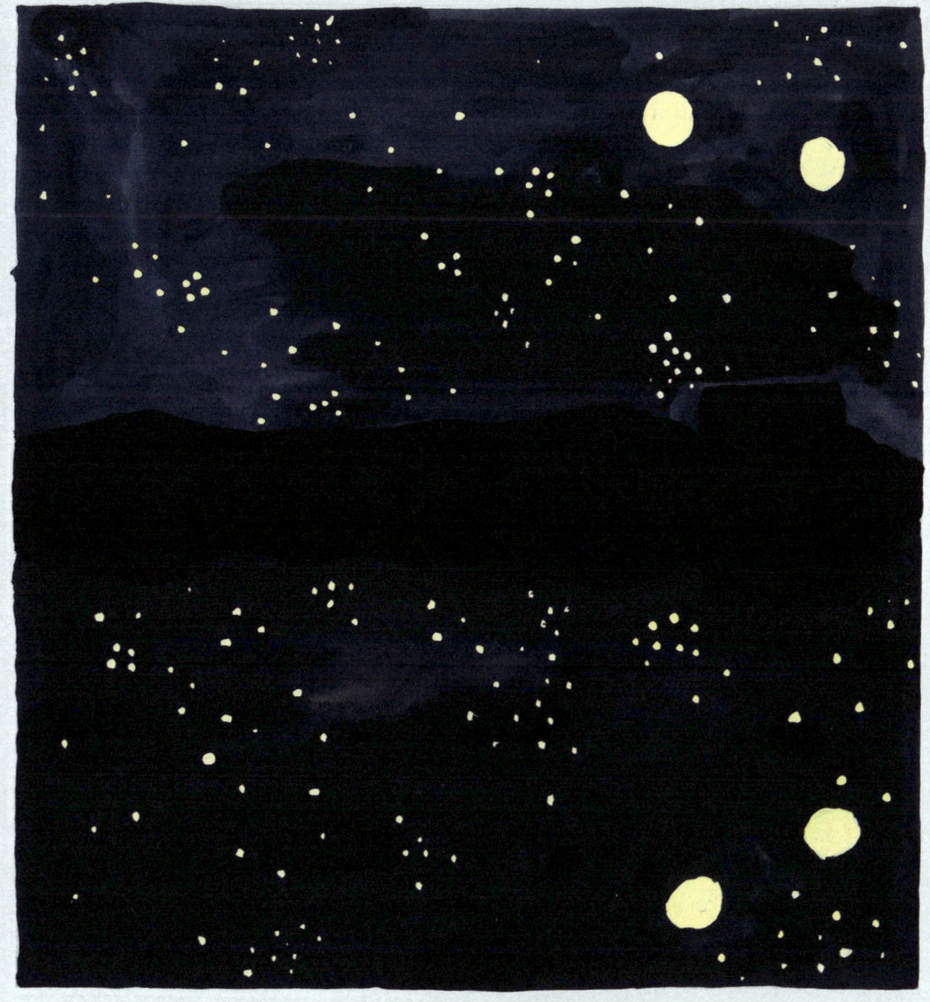

THE HOGARTH PRESS

AND THE INSTITUTE OF PSYCHO-ANALYSIS

THE STANDARD EDITION

OF THE COMPLETE PSYCHOLOGICAL WORKS OF

RROSE NOSER

VOLUME XV

(1915–1916)

Tongues and Armpits

In Collaboration with

ANNA FREUD

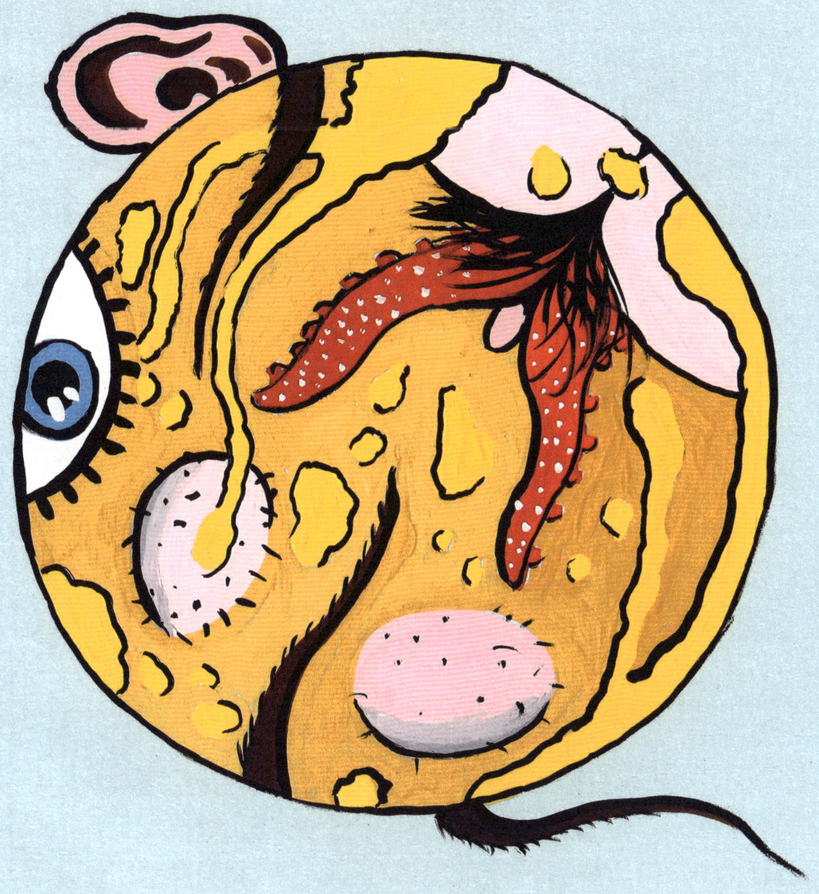

T O T SS

AN STITUT O O SS

THE SATAN EDITION
OF THE COMPLETE PSYCHOLOGICAL WORKS OF

RUSS NERO

VOLUME XVI

(1916–1917)

The Complete History of Russia in Jokes

Incomplete

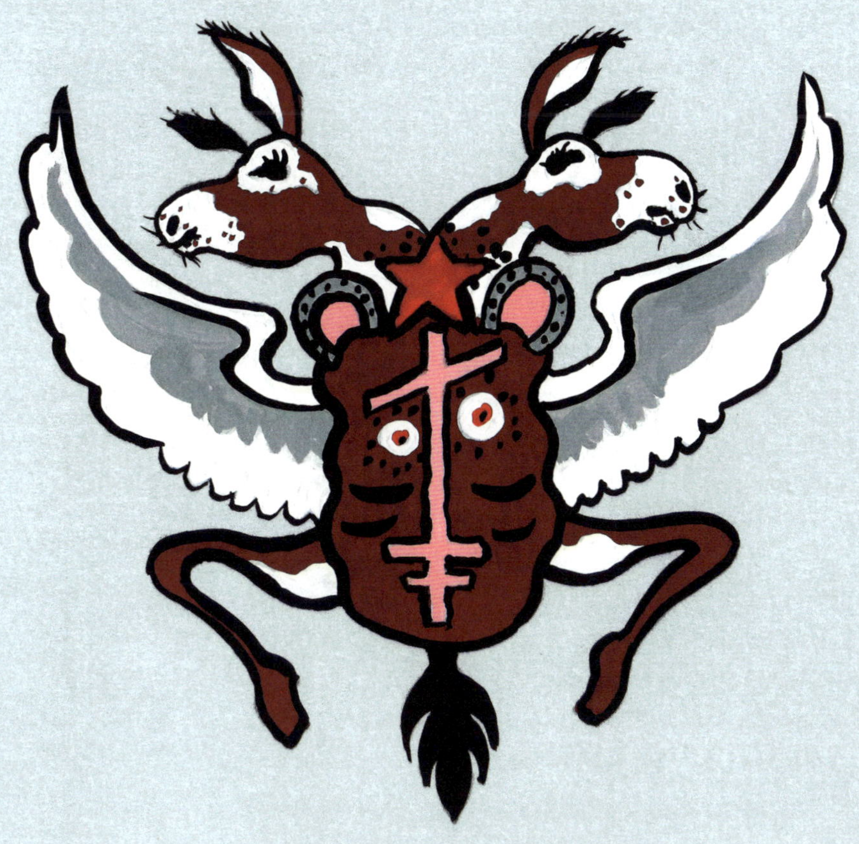

THE HOGARTH PRESS

THE STANDARD EDITION
OF THE COMPLETE PSYCHOLOGICAL WORKS OF

ONAN ARSON

VOLUME XVII
(1917–1919)

The Tribes of My Room

A Pandemic Quarantine Edition

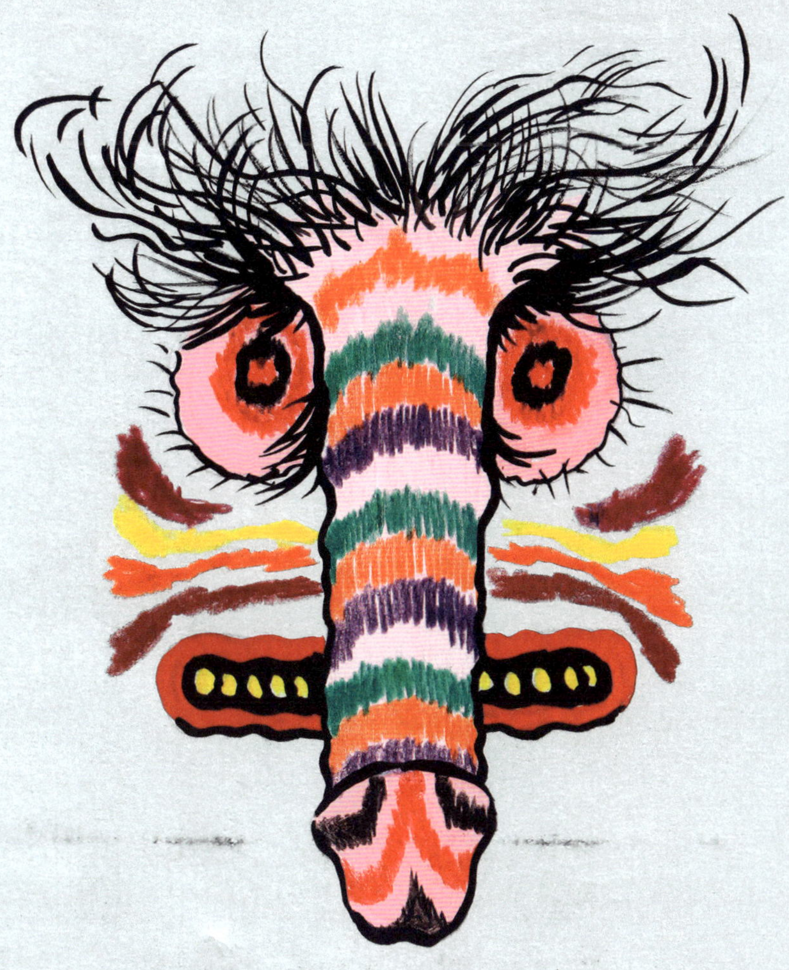

THE INSTITUTE OF PSYCHO-ANALYSIS

THE STANDARD EDITION

SSORERROSEN

VOLUME XVIII

(1920–1922)

How to Hide Your Pains From Yourself

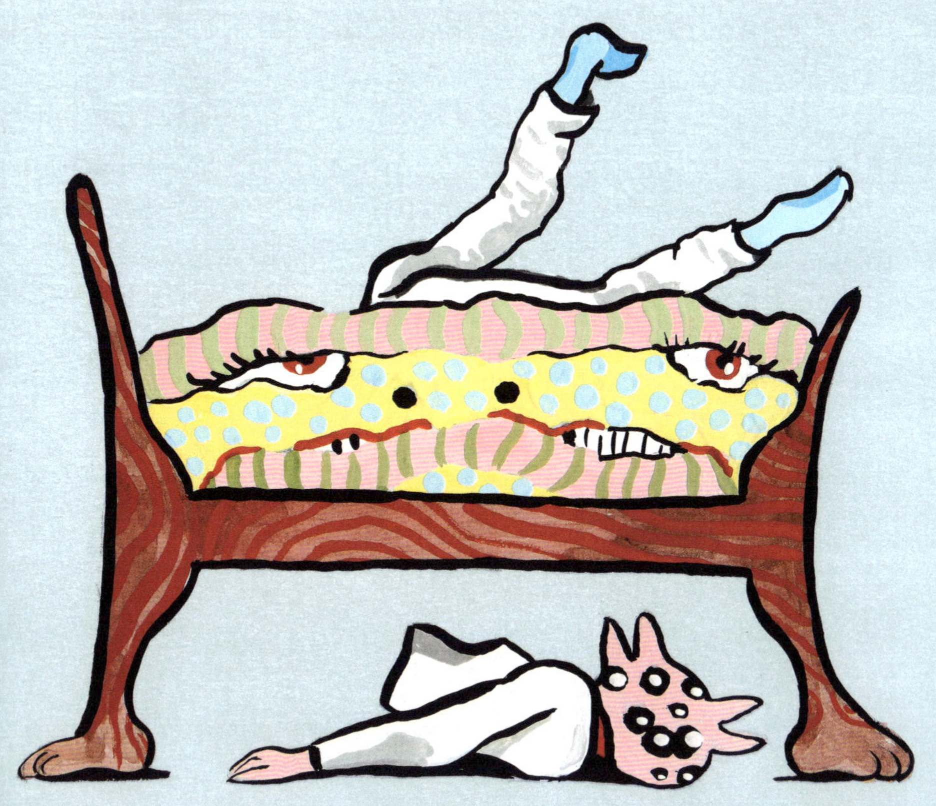

THE PRESS

THE STANDARD EDITION
OF THE COMPLETE PSYCHOLOGICAL WORKS

ORION SEER

VOLUME XIX
(1923–1925)

The Kafka Companion to Wellness

with an Appendix on His Death

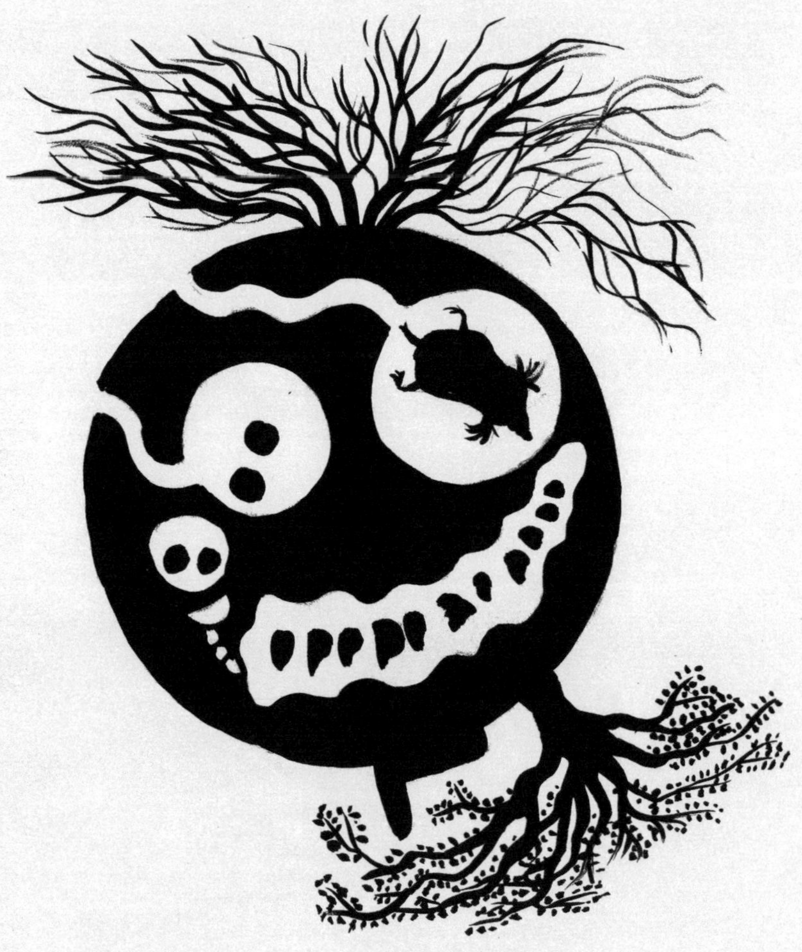

THE HOGARTH PRESS
AND THE INSTITUTE OF NUDE NUTRITION

MORT TERROR

VOLUME XX

(1925–1926)

The Unattainable Ideal of Becoming Ever Smaller

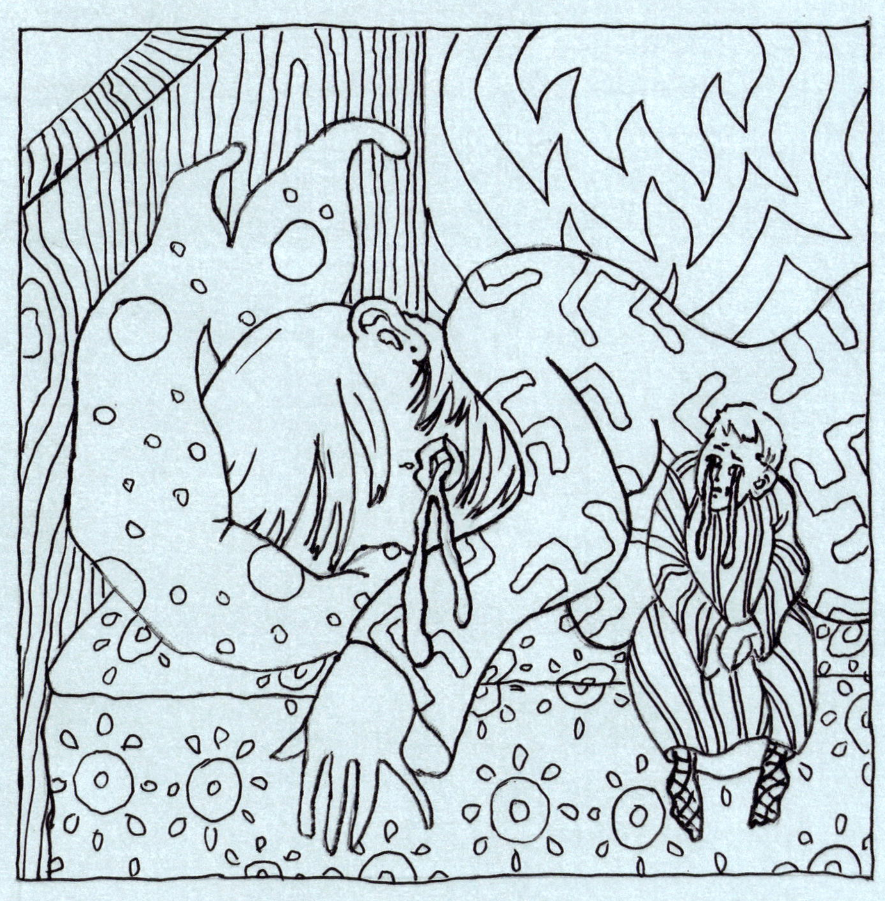

o

o o o o o o

O O

o *o* *o*

o *o* *o*

o

o

(1927–1931)

o o o

O

o o o

o o

o o

O

o o

THE STANDARD EDITION
OF THE COMPLETE PSYCHOLOGICAL WORKS OF

RROSE RRIP

VOLUME XXII

(1932–1936)

How They Took Her from the Playground, Leaving the Children Behind, Unaware

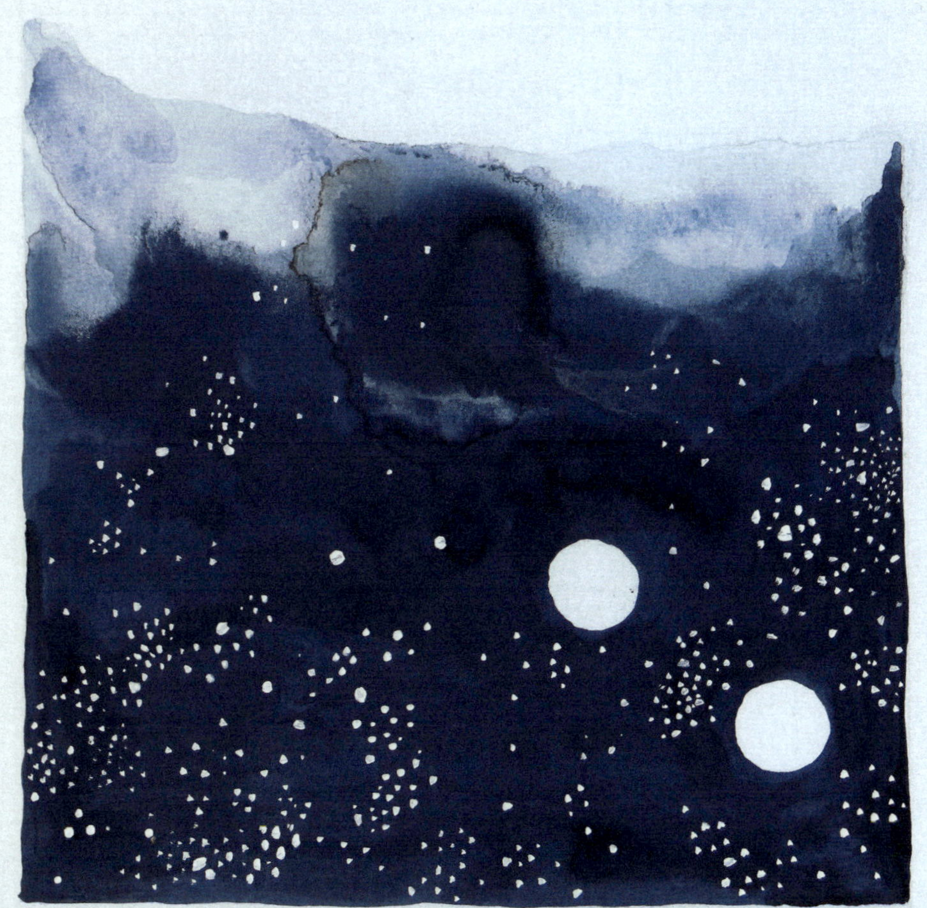

THE STANDARD EDITION
OF THE COMPLETE PSYCHOLOGICAL WORKS OF

ROEE ROSEN

VOLUME XXIII

(1937–1939)

The Horror of Becoming a Frog Again

on Curses and Remissions

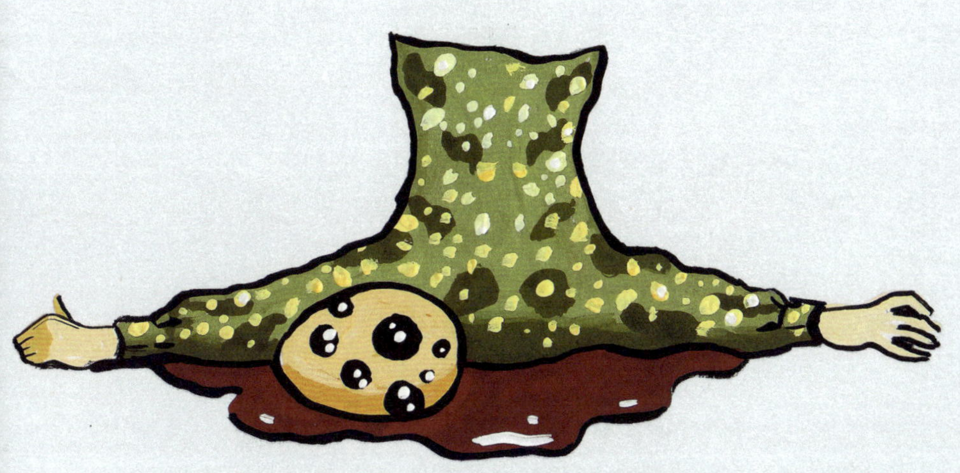

O O

O O

a a *o o*

o o

o a

o o o o

o o

o o

Colophon

This artist book is published on the occasion of the exhibition *Roee Rosen: The Kafka Companion to Wellness* at Kunstverein Hannover, November 9, 2024–January 12, 2025.

Editor
Christoph Platz-Gallus for Kunstverein Hannover

Co-Edited by
Krzysztof Kosciuczuk

Concept
Roee Rosen, Krzysztof Kosciuczuk, Christoph Platz-Gallus

Design
Jasper Otto Eisenecker

Text
Krzysztof Kosciuczuk, Christoph Platz-Gallus

Translation
Henriette Gallus

Copy Editing
Jill Winder, Martin Hager

Image Editing
Carsten Humme, www.humme.com

Production Management
Rebecca Wilton, DISTANZ Verlag

Printing and Binding
Gutenberg Beuys, Langenhagen

ISBN 978-3-95476-684-0
Printed in Germany

Published by
DISTANZ Verlag, www.distanz.de

Kunstverein Hannover is institutionally supported by the Cultural Office of the City of Hannover and Hannover Re Foundation.

The exhibition was kindly supported by the Ministry for Science and Culture of Lower Saxony (MWK), NORD/LB Cultural Foundation, Hannover Re Foundation, VHV Foundation, Hollweg Foundation, as well as Artis and Rosenfeld Gallery.

The educational program is supported by the Ministry for Science and Culture of Lower Saxony (MWK), VGH Foundation, Sparkasse Hannover, and Hörregion Hannover.

DISTANZ

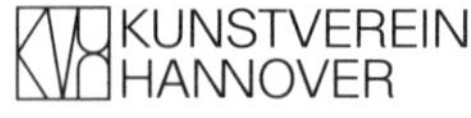

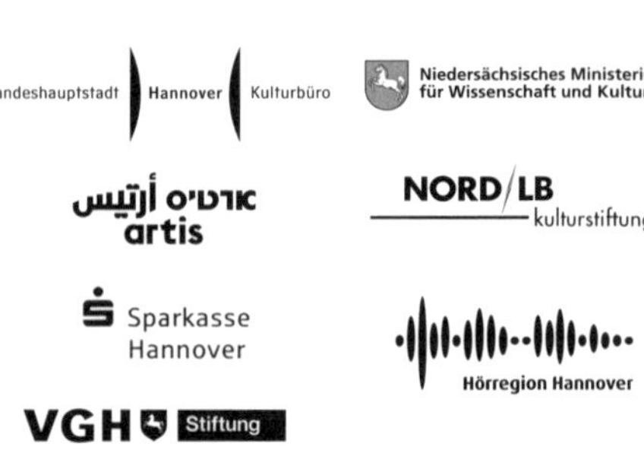

ERRATUM

Einführung auf Deutsch

Die *Sigmund Freud Gesamtausgabe* umfasst 23 Bände der Schriften von Sigismund Schlomo Freud, der am 6. Mai 1856 in Freiberg in Mähren, damals Teil des Kaisertums Österreich, heute Příbor in der Tschechischen Republik, geboren wurde und am 23. September 1939 in London, der Hauptstadt des Vereinigten Königreichs Großbritannien und Nordirland, starb.

Die *Sigmund Freud Gesamtausgabe* der vollständigen psychologischen Werke von Sigmund Freud, gemeinhin als SFG bezeichnet, erschien ab 2015 und umfasst die *Studienausgabe* erweitert um die voranalytischen Schriften Freuds, die weder in selbiger noch in den *Gesammelten Werken* enthalten waren.

Die *Standardausgabe*, die Sie in Händen halten, ist das Ergebnis der Arbeit von Roee Rosen, geboren 1963 in der Stadt Rehovot, etwa zwanzig Kilometer von Tel Aviv-Jaffa in Israel entfernt. Sie wird vom Distanz Verlag und dem Kunstverein Hannover herausgegeben, initiiert von Christoph Platz-Gallus und Krzysztof Kosciuczuk, die alle keinen Anspruch auf die außergewöhnlichen Ergebnisse der Arbeit von Herrn Roee Rosen erheben, außer dass sie sich geehrt fühlen, sie zu veröffentlichen und der Öffentlichkeit zugänglich zu machen. Alle Genannten sind zum Zeitpunkt der Drucklegung noch am Leben, bei Verstand und erfreuen sich eines intakten Erinnerungsvermögens.

Vielleicht ist das Einzige, was wir zu sagen wagen, Folgendes: Die Zeiten ändern sich, Imperien entstehen und fallen, undobwohl es beruhigend ist, das flackernde Licht eines Leuchtturms inmitten des Sturms zu sehen, ist es angebracht, sich nicht mit absolutem Vertrauen darauf zu verlassen. Die Schriften des verehrten Herrn Freud werden von Leserinnen und Lesern auf der ganzen Welt hochgeschätzt. Hier liegt eine andere Sammlung von Werken vor, aus der eine andere Biografie hervorgeht. Dies sind die Bücher, die nie geschrieben wurden. Sie brauchen die Vorstellungskraft der Lesenden, um zum Leben erweckt zu werden. Dies hier ist die Einladung zu Reisen in Länder, die keine Leuchttürme haben.

Die Originalbände der *Sigmund Freud Gesamtausgabe* (SFG) sind folgendermaßen betitelt und editiert:

Band 1-4: Die voranalytischen Schriften (1877–1894)
Band 5: Studien über Hysterie u. a. (1895–1896)
Band 6: Die Sexualität in der Ätiologie der Neurosen u. a. (1897–1900)
Band 7: Die Traumdeutung (1900)
Band 8: Zur Psychopathologie des Alltagslebens u. a. (1901)
Band 9: Der Witz und seine Beziehung zum Unbewußten u. a. (1903–1905)
Band 10: Drei Abhandlungen zur Sexualtheorie, Bruchstück einer Hysterie-Analyse u. a. (1905–1906)
Band 11: Die „kulturelle" Sexualmoral und die moderne Nervosität u. a. (1907–1909)
Band 12: Über Psychoanalyse u. a. (1910–1912)
Band 13: Totem und Tabu u. a. (1913)
Band 14: Der Moses des Michelangelo, Zeitgemäßes über Krieg und Tod u. a. (1914–1916)
Band 15: Vorlesungen zur Einführung in die Psychoanalyse (1916–1917)
Band 16: Trauer und Melancholie, Das Unheimliche u. a. (1917–1920)
Band 17: Jenseits des Lustprinzips, Massenpsychologie und Ich-Analyse, Das Ich und das Es u. a. (1920–1923)
Band 18: Die Frage der Laienanalyse, Die Zukunft einer Illusion u. a. (1924–1927)
Band 19: Das Unbehagen in der Kultur, Neue Folge der Vorlesungen zur Einführung in die Psychoanalyse u. a. (1928–1933)
Band 20: Der Mann Moses und die monotheistische Religion u. a. (1934–1939)
Band 21: Vorträge und Interviews (1886–1938)
Band 22: Freud-Diarium (2 Halbbände): Chroniken, Kalender, Biografisches (1886–1939)
Band 23: Gesamtregister